Terry Tutton

A Voice Crying

in the Wilderness

A VOICE CRYING IN THE WILDERNESS

(Vox Clamantis in Deserto)

Notes from a Secret Journal

EDWARD ABBEY

Illustrations by Andrew Rush

St. Martin's Press / New York

Originally published in 1989 as *Vox Clamantis in Deserto* by the Rydal
Press of Santa Fe, New Mexico, Clark Kimball, publisher, in a first
limited slipcase edition.

Library of Congress Cataloging-in-Publication Data

Abbey, Edward.
        A voice crying in the wilderness-Vox clamantis in deserto /
    Edward Abbey.
            p.   cm.
        ISBN 0-312-04147-0
        1. Aphorisms and apothegms. I. Title. II Title : Vox clamantis
    in deserto.
    PS3551.B2V6 1990
    818'.5402—dc20   89-70251
                                                                  CIP

To my parents,
Mildred and Paul Abbey,
my brothers
John, Howard and Bill,
and my sister
Nancy.

I write to make a difference. "It is always a writer's duty to make the world better," said Samuel Johnson. Distrusting all answers, to raise more questions. To give pleasure and promote esthetic bliss. To honor life and praise the divine beauty of the world. For the joy and exultation of writing itself. To tell my story.

"Well now," says the old wolf, *vox clamantis in deserto*, "that should keep him busy for a while."

—E.A.

CONTENTS

AN INTRODUCTION

It is with considerable diffidence and in the spirit of true humility which only a modern American writer can summon to the page so easily that I hereby offer this pretentious and artistically crafted little volume to the literary public. For years, I have been threatening that public—my readers—such as it is, with the detonation of a Fat Masterpiece. This book, readers, you will be relieved to learn, is not that book. My *Vox* is not fat, not masterly, not even a piece, but a deliberate collocation of fragments.

Most of the statements in the above paragraph are false. Not all of them.

The above statement is false.

In truth, I'm happy to see my *Vox* emerge from its shell, and cannot imagine any pretext for an apology. (A cheap paperback edition will follow in due time.) The shell, in this case, consists of a private journal I've been keeping, fairly faithfully, since 1948; a journal now twenty-one volumes long, and this chick, the bird or book, is simply a collection of fragments from that twenty-one-year-old personal record.

The fragments, or notes, were obviously not chosen at random but with an eye to propositions and declarations that say something provocative in a minimum number of words. I've always been an admirer of the epigram and the aphoristic style— from Montaigne: "It is good to be born in a depraved time; for, compared to others, you gain a reputation for virtue at a small cost." From Schopenhauer: "Style is the physiognomy of the mind," to Samuel Johnson: "Of all forms of wealth, intelligence at least seems fairly distributed; for no man complains of a lack of it." Back to Schopenhauer: "A pessimist is an optimist in full possession of the facts." And on to Ambrose Bierce: "Love is a disease for which marriage is the perfect cure." And George Santayana: "For good or ill I am an ignorant man, almost a poet." And finally, Aristotle: "Melancholy men, of all others, are the most witty." Some of my favorite books, such as Thoreau's *Walden,* can be read as a mosaic of epigrams.

Herewith, I try my hand at it, making no claims at wit or wisdom, but hoping nonetheless (in secret) that within this paper bin the reader may discover a few nuggets of genuine gold, or of that which glitters even better: fool's gold.

Some of these notes have appeared, in altered

form, in previous books of mine, floating along in a flood of earnest prose. Others may be unconscious plagiarisms from the great and dead (never steal from the living and mediocre), ideas absorbed in my reading so long ago that I've made them mine and forgotten the source. If so, the author would appreciate hearing from readers on this point. (Be kind.)

Good or bad, I like to think of these selected journal notes as potential essays, germinal essays, essays in a nutshell—one-liner or one-paragraph monographs—in which some vast formidable thesis, together with resounding conclusion, bristling from end to end with a full armament of *apparatus scholasticus,* is presented in nuclear form, leaving to the reader's discernment, learning, logic, and intellectual energy its unfolding and full development.

An isolate voice, crying from the desert.

Vox clamantis in deserto is a role that few care to play, but I find pleasure in it. The voice crying from the desert, with its righteous assumption of enlightenment, tends to grate on the nerves of the multitude. But it is mine. I've had to learn to live within a constant blizzard of abuse from book reviewers, literary critics, newspaper columnists, letter writers, and fellow authors. But there are some rewards as well: The immense satisfaction, for example, of speaking out in plain blunt language on matters that the majority of American authors are too tired, timid, or temporizing even to allow themselves to think about. To challenge the taboo—that has always been a special delight of mine—and though all respectable and official and institutional voices condemn me, a million others think otherwise and continue to buy my books, paying my bills and financing my primrose path over the hill and down the far side to an early grave. Yes, it's true by God, whatever I've accomplished as a writer, I've done on my own, without any encouragement from my "fellow" authors and against first the indifference and then the resolute opposition of the guardians of our contemporary Kultur.

Kultur, I say, not civilization; when or where has a true civilization, worthy of the respect of honest men and honorable women, ever existed? Name me one organized human society, ethnic group, race, or nation, modern or historic, that does not deserve—on due consideration—our most generous contempt. A few exceptions come to mind: perhaps the Finns, the bushmen of the Kalahari, the Hopi of Arizona—those who have committed least evil in the world; but they are few indeed and they come from the remotest fringes of the anthropocentered hive—in so far as they still exist at all.

This sort of talk is called cranky, cantankerous, misanthropic. I have been called a curmudgeon, which my obsolescent dictionary defines as a "surly, ill-mannered, bad-tempered fellow." The etymology of the word is obscure; in fact, unknown. But through frequent recent usage, the term is acquiring a broader meaning, which our dictionaries have not yet caught up to. Nowadays, curmudgeon is likely to refer to anyone who hates hypocrisy, cant, sham, dogmatic ideologies, the pretenses and evasions of euphemism, and has the nerve to point out unpleasant facts and takes the trouble to impale these sins on the skewer of humor and roast them over the fires of empiric fact, common sense, and native intelligence. In this nation of bleating sheep and braying jackasses, it then becomes an honor to be labeled curmudgeon. I accept the sneer with pleasure, as I would an honorary degree in roach control from the University of . . . well, Ockham. (The razor, William, the razor! No multiplication of superfluous entities!)

The *Deserto* in the title, therefore, denotes not the regions of dry climate and low rainfall on our pillaged planet but, rather, the arid wastes of our contemporary techno-industrial greed-and-power culture; not the clean outback lands of sand, rock, cactus, buzzard, and scorpion, but, rather, the barren neon wilderness and asphalt jungle of the modern urbanized nightmare in which New Age man, eyes hooded, ears plugged, nerves drugged, cannot even get a decent night's sleep. While the grumbling, eccentric *Vox*, though isolated, may speak—I suspect—for the desperations and aspirations of many. Of very many, deprived by circumstance of the opportunity to speak for themselves. Where the means of communication fall within the control of a tightly centralized monopoly, free speech becomes a meaningless gesture, a useless privilege. When and if the opportunity does come, one must make the most of it or betray both thy neighbors and thyself.

So: This, reader, is an honest book. (Never mind the occasional self-contradictions.) It warns you at the outset that my sole purpose has been a private and egocentric one. I have no thought of serving others; such ambition is beyond both my intention and my powers. I am myself the substance of my book. There is no reason why you should waste your leisure on so frivolous and unrewarding a subject. Farewell then, from Abbey, on the parapet of the tower at Fort Llatikcuf, Arizona, in this windblown, dust-obscured midday twilight on this third day of March in the year 1989 anno Domini.

E.A.
March 3, 1989
Fort Llatikcuf, Arizona

A Voice Crying

in the Wilderness

A man without passion would be like a body without a soul. Or even more grotesque, like a soul without a body.

CHAPTER 1

Philosophy, Religion, and So Forth

A good philosopher is one who does not take ideas seriously.

If the world is irrational, we can never know it—either it or its irrationality.

The world is full of burled and gnarly knobs on which you can hang a metaphysical system.
If you must.

The more fantastic an ideology or theology, the more fanatic its adherents.

The missionaries go forth to Christianize the savages—as if the savages weren't dangerous enough already.

If the end does not justify the means—what can?

Reason has seldom failed us because it has seldom been tried.

Is there a God? Who knows? Is there an angry unicorn on the dark side of the moon?

Whatever we cannot easily understand we call God; this saves much wear and tear on the brain tissues.

Who needs astrology? The wise man gets by on fortune cookies.

Jesus don't walk on water no more; his feet leak.

Belief in God? An afterlife? I believe in rock: this apodictic rock beneath my feet.

Preacher to me: "A dollar for the Lord, brother?" Me to preacher: "That's all right, I'm headed his way. I'll give it to him when I see him."

It may be true that there are no atheists in foxholes. But you don't find many Christians there, either. Or, about as many of one as the other.

Christian theology: nothing so grotesque could possibly be true.

Only a fool is astonished by the foolishness of humankind.

I hate intellectual discussion. When I hear the words *phenomenology* or *structuralism,* I reach for my buck knife.

A VOICE CRYING IN THE WILDERNESS

When I hear the word *culture,* I reach for
my checkbook.

From the point of view of a tapeworm, man was
created by God to serve the appetite of
the tapeworm.

What's the difference between the Lone Ranger
and God? There really is a Lone Ranger.

Why do I live in the desert? Because the desert is
the *locus Dei.*

The axiom of conditioned repetition, like the bino-
mial theorem, is nothing but a piece of insolence.

Do I believe in ghosts? I believe in the ghosts that
haunt the human mind.

What did Jesus say to the headwaiter at the Last
Supper? "Separate checks, please."

Every analysis leaves a residue of the unknown;
this we call God or Karma or—depending on time
and place—the UFO. (Unidentified
Fucking Object).

Every man has two vocations: his own
and philosophy.

4

Through logic and inference we can prove anything. Therefore, logic and inference, in contrast to ordinary daily living experience, are secondary instruments of knowledge. Probably tertiary.

Proverbs save us the trouble of thinking. What we call folk wisdom is often no more than a kind of expedient stupidity.

In my case, saving the world was only a hobby.

Appearance *versus* reality? Appearance *is* reality, God damn it!

In both metaphysics and art, honesty is the best policy. Keep it clean.

Every man should be his own guru; every woman her own gurette.

The gurus come from the sickliest nation on earth to tell us how to live. And we pay them for it.

Mormonism: Nothing so hilarious could possibly be true. Or all bad.

Nothing could be more reckless than to base one's moral philosophy on the latest pronouncements of science.

My cousin Elroy spent seven years as an IBM taper staring at THINK signs on the walls before he finally got a good idea: He quit.

My computer tells me that in twenty-five years there will be no more computers.

We are all ONE, say the gurus. Aye, I might agree—but one WHAT?

Fantastic doctrines (like Christianity or Islam or Marxism) require unanimity of belief. One dissenter casts doubt on the creed of millions. Thus the fear and the hate; thus the torture chamber, the iron stake, the gallows, the labor camp, the psychiatric ward.

God is Love? Not bloody likely.

Belief? What do I believe in? I believe in sun. In rock. In the dogma of the sun and the doctrine of the rock. I believe in blood, fire, woman, rivers, eagles, storm, drums, flutes, banjos, and broom-tailed horses. . . .

In metaphysics, the notion that earth and all that's on it is a mental construct is the product of people who spend their lives inside rooms. It is an indoor philosophy.

Metaphysics is a cobweb that the mind weaves around things.

7

Orthodoxy is a relaxation of the mind accompanied by a stiffening of the heart.

According to the current doctrines of mystico-scientism, we human animals are really and actually nothing but "organic patterns of nodular energy composed of collocations of infinitesimal points oscillating on the multi-dimensional coordinates of the space-time continuum. I'll have to think about that. Sometime. Meantime, I'm going to gnaw on this sparerib, drink my Blatz beer, and contemplate the *à posteriori* coordinates of that young blonde over yonder, the one in the tennis skirt, tying her shoelaces.

Belief in the supernatural reflects a failure of
the imagination.

The absurd vanity of metaphysicians who like to
imagine that they create the world by thinking
about it.

The world is older and bigger than we are. This is a
hard truth for some folks to swallow.

When the philosopher's argument becomes tedious, complicated, and opaque, it is usually a sign that he is attempting to prove as true to the intellect what is plainly false to common sense. But men of intellect will believe anything—if it appeals to their ego, their vanity, their sense of self-importance.

I always write with my .357 magnum handy. Why? Well, you never know when God may try to interfere.

I do not believe in personal immortality; it seems so unnecessary. Show me one man who deserves to live forever.

Reply to Plato: I seen horses I seen cows I haint never yet seen horsiness nor that there bovinity neither.

What ideal, immutable Platonic cloud could equal the beauty and perfection of any ordinary everyday cloud floating over, say, Tuba City, Arizona, on a hot day in June?

Zen: the sound of the ax chopping. Chopping logic.

The function of an ideal is not to be realized but, like that of the North Star, to serve as a guiding point.

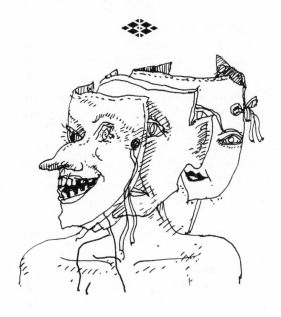

This world may be only illusion—but it's the only illusion we've got.

Is a mirage real? Well, it's a real mirage.

Truth is merely common sense, say the naïve realist. Really? Then where, precisely, is the location of—a rainbow? In the air? In the eye? In between? Or somewhere else?

Only a fool would leave the enjoyment of rainbows to the opticians. Or give the science of optics the last word on the matter.

It may be true that my desk here is really "nothing but" a transient eddy of electrons in the flux of universal process. Nevertheless, I find that it continues to support my feet, my revolver, and my cigars all day long. What happens when my back is turned I don't know. Or much care. That's no concern of mine.

All is One? But One is so Many!

The basic question is this: Why should *anything* exist? *Nothing* would be tidier.

Koan: Why *did* the chicken cross the road?

Better a cruel truth than a comfortable delusion.

A man without passion would be like a body without a soul. Or even more grotesque, like a soul without a body.

What is the purpose of the giant sequoia tree? The purpose of the giant sequoia tree is to provide shade for the tiny titmouse.

We live in a time of twin credulities: the hunger
for the miraculous combined with a servile awe of
science. The mating of the two gives us superstition
plus scientism—a Mongoloid metaphysic.

There is science, logic, reason; there is thought ver-
ified by experience. And then there is California.

Beware the writer who always encloses the word *reality* in quotation marks: He's trying to slip
something over on you. Or into you.

I believe in nothing that I cannot touch, kiss,
embrace. . . . The rest is only hearsay.

The earth is real. Only a fool, milking his cow,
denies the cow's reality.

We should restore the practice of dueling. It might improve manners around here.

CHAPTER 2

Good Manners

Humility is a virtue when you have no other.

Charity should be spontaneous. Calculated altruism
is an affront.

I would never betray a friend to serve a cause.
Never reject a friend to help an institution. Great
nations may fall in ruin before I would sell a friend
to save them.

Beware of the man who has no enemies.

Of all bores, the worst is the sparkling bore.

A VOICE CRYING IN THE WILDERNESS

Farting is such sweet sorrow.

The most striking thing about the rich is the gracious democracy of their manners—and the crude vulgarity of their way of life.

Is the Archbishop's blessing any more meaningful than the Politician's handshake? They come, they go, with bigger things than us on their minds.

We should restore the practice of dueling. It might improve manners around here.

In America, as elsewhere, the general irritability level keeps rising.

There are two kinds of people I cannot abide: bigots and any well-organized ethnic group.

Never eat at a place called Mom's. Never play cards with a man called Doc. Never make love to a woman called Mizz *La Belle Dame.*

I'm a fastidious sort of fellow, fond of watermelon and buckbrush nuts.

Fire lookout, 1400 hours, ferocious lightning storm. Me and God. That fucker is trying to get me again, God damn him. But I got me old .357. . . .

GOOD MANNERS

There's nothing so obscene and depressing as an American Christmas.

Cold morning on Aztec Peak Fire Lookout. First, build fire in old stove. Second, start coffee. Then, heat up last night's pork chops and spinach for breakfast. Why not? And why the hell not?

Nobody seems more obsessed by diet than our anti-materialist, otherworldly, New Age, spiritual types. But if the material world is merely illusion, an honest guru should be as content with Budweiser and bratwurst as with raw carrot juice, tofu, and seaweed slime.

Tofu and futons. The adepts of Orientalism seem to spend most of their lives reclining. They can't quite summon the energy to crawl up onto a chair. Even their Yogic exercises are carried out in a prone or sitting position.

The New Age orgy: The flesh was willing but the spirits weak.

The distrust of wit is the beginning of tyranny.

CHAPTER 3

Government and Politics

In history-as-politics, the "future" is that vacuum
in time waiting to be filled with the antics
of statesmen.

No man is wise enough to be another man's master.
Each man's as good as the next—if not a damn
sight better.

A patriot must always be ready to defend his
country against his government.

All forms of government are pernicious, including
good government.

Some of my ancestors fought in the American Revolution. A few wore red coats, a few wore blue coats, and the rest wore no coats at all. We never did figure out who won that war.

Grown men do not need leaders.

Democracy—rule by the people—sounds like a fine thing; we should try it sometime in America.

The ideal society can be described, quite simply, as that in which no man has the power or means to coerce others.

All power rests on hierarchy: An army is nothing but a well-organized lynch mob.

The true, unacknowledged purpose of capital pun-
ishment is to inspire fear and awe—fear and awe of
the State.

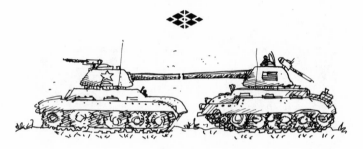

All governments require enemy governments.

The best cure for the ills of democracy is
more democracy.

The purpose and function of government is not to
preside over change but to prevent change. By political methods when unavoidable, by violence
when convenient.

If guns are outlawed, only the government will
have guns.

Society is like a stew. If you don't keep it stirred
up, you get a lot of scum on top.

The distrust of wit is the beginning of tyranny.

No tyranny is so irksome as petty tyranny: the officious demands of policemen, government clerks, and electromechanical gadgets.

Hierarchical institutions are like giant bulldozers—
obedient to the whim of any fool who takes
the controls.

Civilization, like an airplane in flight, survives only
as it keeps going forward.

Anarchism is not a romantic fable but the hard-
headed realization, based on five thousand years of
experience, that we cannot entrust the management
of our lives to kings, priests, politicians, generals,
and county commissioners.

The Old Left: "I like New York," she said, "because there I feel close to the masses."

Anarchy works. Italy has proved it for a thousand years.

The tragedy of modern war is not so much that the young men die but that they die fighting each other—instead of their real enemies back home in the capitals.

Anarchism is founded on the observation that since few men are wise enough to rule themselves, even fewer are wise enough to rule others.

Liberty cannot be guaranteed by law. Nor by anything else except the resolution of free citizens to defend their liberties.

The nuclear bomb took all the fun out of war.

In the Soviet Union, government controls industry. In the United States, industry controls government. That is the principal structural difference between the two great oligarchies of our time.

War: First day in the U.S. Army, the government placed a Bible in my left hand, a bayonet in the other.

All revolutions have failed? Perhaps. But rebellion for good cause is self-justifying—a good in itself. Rebellion transforms slaves into human beings, if only for an hour.

Whenever I read *Time* or *Newsweek* or such magazines, I wash my hands afterward. But how to wash off the small but odious stain such reading leaves on the mind?

The sense of justice springs from self-respect; both are coeval with our birth. Children are born with an innate sense of justice; it usually takes twelve years of public schooling and four more years of college to beat it out of them.

We live in a society in which it is normal to be sick; and sick to be abnormal.

As war and government prove, insanity is the most contagious of diseases.

Men love their ideas more than their lives. And the more preposterous the idea, the more eager they are to die for it. And to kill for it.

Nothing can excel a few days in jail for giving a young man or woman a quick education in the basis of industrial society.

GOVERNMENT AND POLITICS

In a nation of sheep, one brave man forms
a majority.

Taxation : how the sheep are shorn.

Our big social institutions do not reflect human
nature ; they distort it.

You cannot reshape human nature without mutilat-
ing human beings.

Recorded history is largely an account of the crimes
and disasters committed by banal little men at the
levers of imperial machines.

Filling out the form : Race? Human. Religion?
Paiute. Occupation? Criminal anarchy. Hobbies?
Survival with honor.

War? The one war I'd be happy to join is the war
against officers.

In social affairs, I'm an optimist. I really do believe that our military-industrial civilization will
soon collapse.

I know my own nation best. That's why I despise it
the most. And know and love my own people, too,
the swine. I'm a patriot. A dangerous man.

The death penalty would be even more effective, as a deterrent, if we executed a few innocent people more often.

Why I oppose the nuclear-arms race: I prefer the human race.

The rifle and handgun are ''equalizers''—the weapons of a democracy. Tanks and bombers represent dictatorship.

The world of employer and employee, like that of master and slave, debases both.

Government: If you refuse to pay unjust taxes, your property will be confiscated. If you attempt to defend your property, you will be arrested. If you resist arrest, you will be clubbed. If you defend yourself against clubbing, you will be shot dead. These procedures are known as the Rule of Law.

The more corrupt a society, the more numerous its laws.

In social institutions, the whole is always less than the sum of its parts. There will never be a state as good as its people, or a church worthy of its congregation, or a university equal to its faculty and students.

Our "neoconservatives" are neither new nor conservative, but old as Babylon and evil as Hell.

Defiance is beautiful. The defiance of power, especially great or overwhelming power, exalts and glorifies the rebel.

"Have a nice day," said Lady Macbeth.

Truth is always the enemy of power. And power the enemy of truth.

Freedom begins between the ears.

27

The "Terror" of the French Revolution lasted for ten years. The terror that preceded and led to it lasted for a thousand years.

King Arthur and his armored goons of the Round Table functioned as the Politburo of a slave state: Camelot. Of all who have written on the Matter of Arthur, from Malory to White, only Mark Twain understood this. But Mark Twain was a great writer.

If, as some say, evil lies in the hearts not the institutions of men, then there's hardly a distinction worth making between, say, Hitler's Germany and Rebecca's Sunnybrook Farm.

Counterpart to the knee-jerk liberal is the new knee-pad conservative, always groveling before the rich and the powerful.

Our contemporary Tories prefer the term *ordered liberty* to *freedom*. The word *freedom* scares them; it has too much of a wild Paleolithic ring to it.

One can imagine a sane, healthy, cheerful human society based on no more than the principles of common sense, as validated each day by work, play, and living experience. But this remains the most utopian and fantastic of ideals.

Power is always dangerous. Power attracts the worst and corrupts the best.

How to Overthrow the System: brew your own beer; kick in your Tee Vee; kill your own beef; build your own cabin and piss off the front porch whenever you bloody well feel like it.

Humankind will not be free until the last Kremlin commissar is strangled with the entrails of the last Pentagon chief of staff.

A true libertarian supports free enterprise, opposes big business; supports local self-government, opposes the nation-state; supports the National Rifle Association, opposes the Pentagon.

Spartacus, like Jesus, was also crucified by the Romans. And for equally good reasons.

J. Edgar Hoover, J. Bracken Lee, J. Parnell Thomas, J. Paul Getty—you can always tell a shithead by that initial initial.

Representative government has broken down. Our politicians represent not the people who vote for them but the commercial interests who finance their election campaigns. We have the best politicians that money can buy.

Might does not make right but it sure makes what is.

Except for the scale of the operation, there was nothing unusual about Hitler's massacre of the Jews. Genocide's an old tradition, as human as mother love or cherry pie.

Government should be weak, amateurish and ridiculous. At present, it fulfills only a third of the role.

If America could be, once again, a nation of self-reliant farmers, craftsmen, hunters, ranchers, and artists, then the rich would have little power to dominate others. Neither to serve nor to rule: That was the American dream.

What's the difference between a whore and a congressman? A congressman makes more money.

Cities should be like the county fairgrounds: empty places except during times of festival and tournament.

Terrorism: deadly violence against humans and other living things, usually conducted by government against its own people.

A leader leads from in front, by the power of example. A ruler pushes from behind, by means of the club, the whip, the power of fear.

I am an enemy of the State. But isn't everyone?

The rebel is doomed to a violent death. The rest of us can look forward to sedated expiration in a coma inside an oxygen tent, with tubes inserted in every bodily orifice.

The one thing worse than a knee-pad Tory is a chickenshit liberal. The type that can not say "shit" even when his mouth is full of it.

All governments need enemies. How else to justify their existence?

I am my brother's keeper, says the chickenshit liberal. Perhaps he does not realize that he now has more than 2½ billion brothers.

GOVERNMENT AND POLITICS

There never was a good war or a bad revolution.

Three words remain that can yet stir the blood of a man : the word *rebellion;* the word *revolt;* the word *revolution.*

There has never yet been a human society worthy of the name of civilization. Civilization remains a remote ideal.

"Say what you like about my bloody murderous government," I says, "but don't insult me poor bleedin' country."

There has got to be a God ; the world could not have become so fucked up by chance alone.

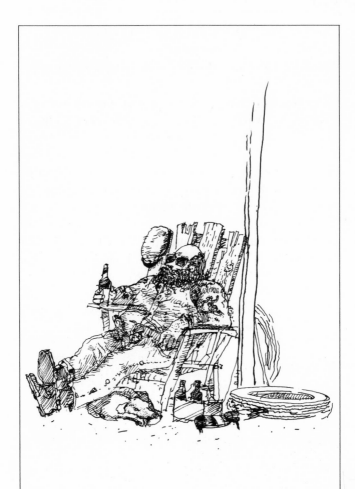

Beauty is only skin deep; ugliness goes all the way through.

CHAPTER 4

Life and Death and All That

The tragic sense of life: our heroic acceptance of the suffering of others.

There has never been an *original* sin: each is quite banal.

The ready availability of suicide, like sex and alcohol, is one of life's basic consolations.

Only the half-mad are wholly alive.

When the situation is hopeless, there's nothing to worry about.

The fear of death follows from the fear of life. A man who lives fully is prepared to die at any time.

A drink a day keeps the shrink away.

Beauty is only skin deep; ugliness goes all the way through.

LIFE AND DEATH AND ALL THAT

Ah, to be a buzzard now that spring is here!

By the age of forty, a man is responsible for his face. And his fate.

A man is not aware of his virtues (if any). Nevertheless, one hopes that they exist.

Life: another day, another dolor.

Suicide: Don't knock it if you ain't tried it.

There are circumstances in which suicide presents a viable option; a workable alternative; the only sensible solution.

I have found through trial and error that I work
best under duress. In fact I work only
under duress.

Home is where, when you have to go there, you
probably shouldn't.

LIFE AND DEATH AND ALL THAT

Is it possible to grow wiser without knowing it?
One hopes so. We all hope so.

Life imitates art—but badly.

For this world that men have made, none of us is
bad enough. For the world that made us, none is
good enough.

Men have never loved one another much, for reasons we can readily understand: Man is not a
lovable animal.

A life without tragedy would not be worth living.

We live in the kind of world where courage is the
most essential of virtues; without courage, the other
virtues are useless.

Longevity, like intelligence and good looks and
health and strength of character, is largely a matter
of genetic heritage. Choose your parents with care.

The best people, like the best wines, come from
the hills.

The consolation of reading biography: Most great
men have led lives even more miserable than
our own.

Sentiment without action is the ruin of the soul. One brave deed is worth a thousand books.

In the modern technoindustrial culture, it is possible to proceed from infancy into senility without ever knowing manhood.

Epitaphs for a gravestone: Please: no hooliganism; or *Es prohibe se hace agua aqui;* or No comment.

LIFE AND DEATH AND ALL THAT

Life without music would be an intolerable insult.

Life is hard? True—but let's love it anyhow, though it breaks every bone in our bodies.

Life is cruel? Compared to what?

The greater your dreams, the more terrible your nightmares.

Beware of your wishes: They will probably come true.

A VOICE CRYING IN THE WILDERNESS

Life is too tragic for sadness: Let us rejoice.

Most of us lead lives of chaotic improvisation from day to day, bawling for peace while plunging grimly into fresh disorders.

Indolence and melancholy: Each generates the other. If one can speak of such feeble passions as generating anything.

If you feel that you must suffer, then plan your suffering carefully—as you choose your dreams, as you conceive your ancestors.

Life is unfair. And it's not fair that life is unfair.

A mother's sorrow is more true, honorable, and beautiful than the detachment of the sage.

It's a fool's life, a rogue's life, and a good life if you keep laughing all the way to the grave.

I have been a lucky man. But someone has to be.

There is a deep, abiding, unshakable satisfaction in a life of complete failure.

Cheer up, comrades: You can't feel as bad as you look. Or look as bad as you feel.

As a confirmed melancholic, I can testify that the best and maybe only antidote for melancholia is *action*. However, like most melancholics, I suffer also from sloth.

Once upon a time, I dreamed of becoming a great man. Later, a good man. Now, finally, I find it difficult enough and honor enough to be—a man.

Desire, said the Buddha, is the cause of suffering. But without desire, what delight?

If my decomposing carcass helps nourish the roots of a juniper tree or the wings of a vulture—that is immortality enough for me. And as much as anyone deserves.

If you feel that you're not ready to die, never fear; nature will give you complete and adequate assistance when the time comes.

I was once invited to take part in a heroic, possibly fatal enterprise, but I declined, mainly on account of sloth.

My Publisher: "Yes, sooner or later, we all wake up dead!"

Some lives are tragic, some ridiculous. Most are both at once.

By the age of eighteen, a human has acquired enough joy and heartache to provide the food of reflection for a century.

My Aunt Ida at age eighty-three: "Yeah," she
said, "I'll be dead pretty soon. And frankly, I
don't give a damn."

Every moment is precious. And precarious.

Paradise for a happy man lies in his own
good nature.

Be of good cheer: We'll yet live to piss on the
graves of our enemies.

How can I be so evil? It ain't easy.

Nobody has so many friends that he can afford to
lose one.

No man likes to be smoked out of his hole
in February.

The great question of life is not the question of
death but the question of life. Fear of death shames
us all.

One must be reasonable in one's demands on life.
For myself, all that I ask is: (1) accurate information; (2) coherent knowledge; (3) deep under-
standing; (4) infinite loving wisdom; and (5) no
more kidney stones, please.

45

Those who fear death most are those who enjoy life least.

I like the smell of oil, grease, gasoline—and gunfire.

One thing worse than self-hatred is chiggers.

Saving the world was merely a hobby. My *vocation* has been that of inspector of desert water holes.

Death is every man's final critic. To die well you must live bravely.

When the situation is desperate, it is too late to be serious. Be playful.

"Welcome to the banquet of life," said a recent Pope, forgetting that most have to fight their way to the table.

Writing on the wall: "Will trade three blind crabs for two with no teeth."

The world is wide and beautiful. But almost everywhere, everywhere, the children are dying.

To the intelligent man or woman, life appears infinitely mysterious. But the stupid have an answer for every question.

One day in Dipstick, Nebraska, or Landfill, Oklahoma, is worth more to me than an eternity in Dante's plastic Paradiso, or Yeats's gold-plated Byzantium.

Let us praise the noble turkey vulture: No one envies him; he harms nobody; and he contemplates our little world from a most serene and noble height.

Love implies anger. The man who is angered by nothing cares about nothing.

There comes a time in the life of us all when we must lay aside our books or put down our tools and leave our place of work and walk forth on the road to meet the enemy face-to-face. Once and for all and at last.

There is a wine called Easy Days and Mellow Nights, well-known on the outskirts of the Navajo reservation. It is an economical wine, fortified with the best of intentions, and I recommend it to every serious wino.

Mental degeneracy may be caused by lead poisoning. Or by a poor dip in the gene pool.

An empty man is full of himself.

Life is too short for grief. Or regret. Or bullshit.

I intend to be good for the rest of my natural life—if I live that long.

We judge individual men and women as we do nations and races—by the character of their achievement and by their achievement of character.

Art, science, philosophy, religion—each offers at best only a crude simplification of actual living experience.

Crossing the bar: "I want to buy a beer for every man in the house. If any."

I find more and more, as I grow older, that I prefer women to men, children to adults, animals to humans. . . . And rocks to living things? No, I'm not that old yet.

Henry James: our finest lady novelist.

CHAPTER 5

On Writing and Writers, Books and Art

I am happy to be a regional writer. My region is the American West, old Mexico, West Virginia, New York, Europe, Australia, the human heart, and the male groin.

The writer speaks not *to* his audience (who wants to listen to lectures?) but *for* them, expressing their thoughts and emotions through the imaginative power of his art.

Literary critics, like a herd of cows or a school of fish, always face in the same direction, obeying that love for unity that every critic requires.

51

In writing, fidelity to fact leads eventually to the poetry of truth.

Any hack can safely rail away at foreign powers beyond the sea; but a good writer is a critic of the society he lives in.

A genius is always on duty; even his dreams are tax deductible.

Jack Kerouac, like a sick refrigerator, worked too hard at keeping cool and died on his mama's lap from alcohol and infantilism.

I would prefer to write about everything; what else is there? But one must be selective.

Remembrance of Things Past: an enormous fruit-cake laced with cyanide.

The Proustian aquarium: grotesque and gorgeous fish drifting with languid fins through a sub-aqueous medium of pale violet polluted ink.

Henry James was our master of periphrasis—the fine art of saying as little as possible in the greatest possible number of words.

There is a kind of poetry in simple fact.

Anywhere, anytime, I'd sacrifice the finest nuance for a laugh, the most elegant trope for a smile.

I've never yet read a review of one of my own books that I couldn't have written much better myself.

"The mind is everything," wrote Proust. No doubt true, when you're dead from the neck down.

Books are like eggs—best when fresh.

The artist's job? To be a miracle worker: make the blind see, the dull feel, the dead to live. . . .

Apuleius married a rich widow, then wrote *The Golden Ass.*

The best thing about graduating from the university was that I finally had time to sit on a log and read a good book.

Most of the literary classics are worth reading, if you've nothing better to do.

Platitude: a statement that denies by implication what it explicitly affirms.

There are only two kinds of books—good books and the others. The good are winnowed from the bad through the democracy of time.

Most writers are naturally sycophants. Born in the fetal position, they never learn to stand erect.

Most new books drop immediately into the oblivion they so richly deserve.

A good book is a kind of paper club, serving to rouse the slumbrous and to silence the obtuse.

Proust again: One can only wish that a man with such powers of total recall had led a less tedious life, moved among somewhat livelier circles. . . .

Henry James: our finest lady novelist.

Jane Austen: Getting into her books is like getting in bed with a cadaver. Something vital is lacking; namely, life.

William Dean Howells: a rubber chicken dangling on a string.

Literature, like anything else, can become a wearisome business if you make a lifetime specialty of it. A healthy, wholesome man would no more spend his entire life reading great books than he would packing cookies for Nabisco.

Poetry—even bad poetry—may be our final hope.

A VOICE CRYING IN THE WILDERNESS

The artist in our time has two chief responsibilities:
(1) art; and (2) sedition.

Romanticism was more than merely an alternative
to a sterile classicism; romanticism made possible,
especially in art, a great expansion of the human
consciousness.

Good writing can be defined as having something to
say and saying it well. When one has nothing to say,
one should remain silent. Silence is always beautiful at such times.

Writers should avoid the academy. When a writer
begins to accept pay for talking about words, we
know what he will produce soon: nothing
but words.

What are called inspirational books, like Gibran's
The Prophet or Bach's *Seagull*, seem to have been
strained through a bowl of fish-eye tapioca.

One word is worth a thousand pictures. If it's the
right word.

The best American writers have come from the hin-
terlands—Mark Twain, Theodore Dreiser, Jack
London, Hemingway, Faulkner, Wolfe, Steinbeck.
Most of them never even went to college.

All serious writers want the obvious rewards: fame, money, women, love—and most of all, an audience!

The writer concerned more with technique than truth becomes a technician, not an artist.

In art as in a boat, a bullet, or a coconut-cream pie, purpose determines form.

When a writer has done the best that he can do, he should then withdraw from the book-writing business and take up an honest trade like shoe repair, cattle stealing, or screwworm management.

There is no trajectory so pathetic as that of an artist in decline.

A shelf of classics for our young adults: Tolkien, Hesse, Casteneda, Kerouac, Salinger, Tom Robbins, and *The Last Whole Earth Catalog*.

When the writer has done his best, he then should proceed to do his second best.

Susan Sontag: What she really wanted, throughout her career, was to grow up to be a Frenchman.

How long does it take to write a good book? All of the years that you've lived.

My own best books have not been published. In fact, they've not even been written yet.

My sole literary ambition is to write one good novel, then retire to my hut in the desert, assume the lotus position, compose my mind and senses, and sink into meditation, contemplating my novel.

A formal education can sometimes be broadening but more often merely flattens.

It is true that some of my fiction was based on actual events. But the events took place after the fiction was written.

My books are not taken seriously. But that's all right; they are given playfully.

Style: There is something in too much verbal felicity (as in Joyce or Nabokov or Borges) that can betray the writer into technique for the sake of technique.

In the world of words, one of my best-loved tribes is the diatribe.

Every writer has his favorite coterie of enemies: Mine is the East Coast literati—those prep school playmates and their Ivy League colleagues.

Salome had but seven veils; the artist has
a thousand.

In the modern world, all literary art is necessarily
political—especially that which pretends not to be.

Desire lends strength. Aspiration creates inspiration, which, for the artist, is the breath of life.

James Joyce buried himself in his great work. *Finnegans Wake* is his monument and his tombstone. A
dead end.

Critics are like ticks on a dog or tits on a motor:
ornamental but dysfunctional.

A critic is to an author as a fungus to an oak.

The response to my books from my East Coast
friends has been wildly various, running the gamut
from "bad" to "very bad." (Is there
another gamut?)

The sneakiest form of literary subtlety, in a corrupt
society, is to speak the plain truth. The critics will
not understand you; the public will not believe
you; your fellow writers will shake their heads.
Laughter, praise, honors, money, and the love of
beautiful girls will be your only reward.

Vladimir Nabokov was a writer who cared nothing for music and whose favorite sport was the pursuit, capture, and murder of butterflies. This explains many things; for example, the fact that Nabokov's novels, for all their elegance and wit, resemble nothing so much as butterflies pinned to a board: pretty but dead; symmetrical but stiff.

It is always dishonest for a reviewer to review the author instead of the author's book.

My notion of a great novel is something like a five-hundred-page shaggy-dog story, with only the punch line omitted.

The ideal kitchen-sink novel: Throw in everything but the kitchen sink. Then add the kitchen sink.

My books always make the best-seller lists in Wolf Hole, Arizona, and Hanksville, Utah.

Some people write to please, to soothe, to console. Others to provoke, to challenge, to exasperate and infuriate. I've always found the second approach the more pleasing.

There is a fine art to making enemies and it requires diligent cultivation. It's not as easy as it looks.

Too many American authors have a servile streak where their backbone should be. Where's our latest Nobel laureate? More than likely you'll find him in the Rose Garden kissing the First Lady's foot.

Perfection is a minor virtue.

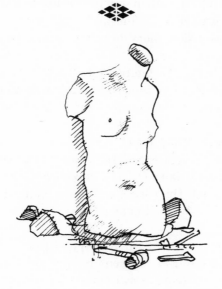

Great art is never perfect; perfect art is never great.

In art as in life, form and subject, body and soul, are one.

John Updike: our greatest suburban chic-boutique man of letters. A smug and fatal complacency has stunted his growth beyond hope of surgical repair. Not enough passion in his collected works to generate steam in a beer can. Nevertheless, he is considered by some critics to be America's finest *living* author: Hold a chilled mirror to his lips and you will see, presently, a fine and dewy moisture condensing—like a faery breath!—upon the glass.

"Be fair," say the temporizers, "tell both sides of the story." But how can you be fair to both sides of a rape? Of a murder? Of a massacre?

Shakespeare wrote great poetry and preposterous plays. Who really cares, for example, which petty tyrant rules Milan? Or who succeeds to the throne of Denmark? Or why the barons ganged up on Richard II?

There comes a point, in literary objectivity, when the author's self-effacement is hard to distinguish from moral cowardice.

Fence straddlers have no balls. In compensation, however, they enjoy a comfortable seat and can retreat swiftly, when danger threatens, to either side of the fence. There is something to be said for every position.

Edmund Wilson was our greatest American literary critic because he was more than a literary critic: He was a fearless, even radical judge of the society he lived in. (See, for example, *A Piece of My Mind; The Cold War and the Income Tax;* the introduction to *Patriotic Gore.*) Our conventional critics cannot forgive him for those scandalous lapses in good taste.

Those art lovers who pride themselves mostly on *taste* usually possess no other talent.

Our suicidal poets (Plath, Berryman, Lowell, Jarrell, et al.) spent too much of their lives inside rooms and classrooms when they should have been trudging up mountains, slogging through swamps, rowing down rivers. The indoor life is the next best thing to premature burial.

It is an author's most solemn obligation to honor truth. If the free and independent writer does not speak truth to power, who will?

There is much to admire in the work of D. H. Lawrence—excepting his queer, soft, gooey, and epicene prose.

In order to write a book, it is necessary to sit down (or stand up) and write. Therein lies the difficulty.

Most of what we call the classics of world literature suggest artifacts in a wax museum. We have to hire and pay professors to get them read and talked about.

Great art is indefinable but that's all right; it exists anyway.

It is not the writer's task to answer questions but to question answers. To be impertinent, insolent, and, if necessary, subversive.

Why the critics, like a flock of ducks, always move in perfect unison: Their authority with the public depends upon an appearance of unanimous agreement. One dissenting voice would shatter the whole fragile structure.

A good writer must have more than vin rosé in his veins, use more than Chablis for ink.

There are two kinds of art: (1) decorative, nonobjective, wallpaper art; and (2) art with a moral purpose.

Why do I write? I write to entertain my friends and to exasperate our enemies. To unfold the folded lie, to record the truth of our time, and, of course, to promote esthetic bliss.

Like any writer, I'd rather be read than dead. Like any serious *author*, I'd rather be dead than not read at all.

The author: an imaginary person who writes real books.

Baseball is a slow, sluggish game, with frequent and trivial interruptions, offering the
spectator many opportunities to reflect at leisure upon the situation on the field: This is
what a fan loves most about the game.

CHAPTER 6

Sport

There's something about winning at poker that restores my faith in the innate goodness of my fellowman.

Football is a game for trained apes. That, in fact, is what most of the players are—retarded gorillas wearing helmets and uniforms. The only thing more debased is the surrounding mob of drunken monkeys howling the gorillas on.

Climbing K-2 or floating the Grand Canyon in an inner tube: There are some things one would rather *have done* than *do*.

Going to bed with Gertrude Stein, Jeane Kirkpatrick, Susan Sontag, or Margaret Thatcher: There are some things one prefers neither to do nor to have done.

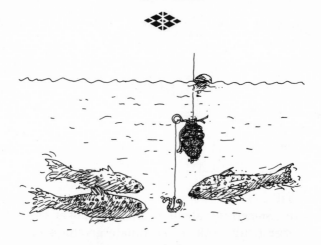

Trout fishing. One must be a stickler for proper form. Use nothing but #4 blasting caps. Or a hand grenade, if handy. Or at a pool well-lined with stone, one blast from a .44 magnum will bring a few stunned brookies quietly to the surface.

Baseball serves as a good model for democracy in action: Every player is equally important and each has a chance to be a hero.

SPORT

Whenever I see a photograph of some sportsman grinning over his kill, I am always impressed by the striking moral and esthetic superiority of the dead animal to the live one.

As between the skulking and furtive poacher, who hunts for the sake of meat, and the honest gentleman shooter, who kills for the pleasure of sport, I find the former a higher type of humanity.

When riding my old Harley at ninety per at midnight down the Via Roma in Naples, I kept one consolation firmly in mind: If anything goes wrong, I'll never have time to regret it.

Baseball is a slow, sluggish game, with frequent and trivial interruptions, offering the spectator many opportunities to reflect at leisure upon the situation on the field: This is what a fan loves most about the game.

The night I filled an inside straight: Even a blind hog's gonna root up an acorn once in a while.

It's true: Every time you kill an elk, you're saving some cow's life.

Tee Vee football: one team wins, one team loses— they tie—who cares? And why?

Simplicity is always a virtue. One kid on a riverbank working out a Stephen Foster tune on his new harmonica heard from the correct esthetic distance projects more magic and power than the entire Vienna Philharmonic and Chorus laboring (once again) through the Mozart Requiem or Bach's B Minor Mass.

CHAPTER 7

Music

Music begins where words leave off. Music expresses the inexpressible. If there is a Kingdom of Heaven, it lies in music.

Music clouds the intellect but clarifies the heart.

How did Haydn and Mozart produce such vast quantities of formally perfect art? They worked from a perfect formula. In music, Beethoven was the Great Emancipator.

If there's anything I hate, it's the vibraphone. And the cha-cha-cha. And Latin rhythms generally.

71

The critics say that Shostakovich's Fourth Symphony has no form. They are wrong; it has the form of Shostakovich's Fourth Symphony.

"Rock" is the music of slaves. Of adolescents pursuing the illusion of freedom and protest while the steel chains of technology bind them ever tighter.

"Rock": music to hammer out fenders by. Music for vomiting to after a hard day spreading asphalt. Vietnam music. Imitation-Afro, industrial air-compressor music.

As Mark Twain said, "I love Wagner—if only they'd cut out all that damned singing!"

Grand opera is a form of musical entertainment for people who hate music.

Opera: I like it, except for all those howling sopranos and caterwauling tenors. (Why can't tenors sing like men?)

Life without music would be an intolerable insult.

A Mahler symphony is full of surprises—but each surprise, on second hearing, turns out to be an *inevitable* surprise.

The best argument for Christianity is the Gregorian chant. Listening to that music, one can believe anything—while the music lasts.

Reincarnation? There is such a thing. What could be more Mozartian than the *Nutcracker* Suite?

Anton Bruckner wrote the same symphony nine times (ten, actually), trying to get it just right. He failed.

Music is a savage art, a measured madness.

Simplicity is always a virtue. One kid on a river-bank working out a Stephen Foster tune on his new harmonica heard from the correct esthetic distance projects more magic and power than the entire Vienna Philharmonic and Chorus laboring (once again) through the Mozart Requiem or Bach's B Minor Mass.

Music endures and ages far better than books. Books, made of words, are unavoidably attached to ideas, events, conflict, and history, but music has the power to transcend time. At least for a time. Palestrina sounds as fresh today as he did in 1555, but Dante, only three centuries older, already smells of the archaic, the medieval, the catacombs.

Mozart, striving for perfection, wrote the same symphony forty-one times. In his case, it worked. He wrote a perfect symphony.

MUSIC

Poor Dimitri Shostakovich: In the Soviet Union, he was condemned as being too radical; in the West, for being too conservative. He could please no one but the musical public. He revenged himself on both by writing a short piece called "March of the Soviet Police."

In the end, for all of our differences and conflicts, most women and men share the same food, work, shelter, bed, life, joy, anguish, and fate. We need each other.

CHAPTER 8

On Women, Love, Sex, Et Cetera

A pretty girl can do no wrong.

In everything but brains and brawn, women are vastly superior to men. A different race.

Free love is priced right.

Married couples who quarrel bitterly every day may really need each other as deeply as those who appear to be desperately in love.

Girls, like flowers, bloom but once. But once is enough.

In marriage, the occasional catastrophic crisis is easier to manage than the daily routine.

I've wrecked and ravaged half my life in the pursuit of women, and I suffer the pangs of about seventeen regrets—the seventeen who got away.

Women: We cannot love them all. But we must try.

Girls: I never wanted them all. Just all the ones I wanted.

I, too, believe in fidelity. But how can I be true to one woman without being false to all the others?

Chastity is more a state of mind than of anatomy.

There has never been a day in my life when I was not in love.

The feminists have a legitimate grievance. But so does everyone else.

It is the difference between men and women, not the sameness, that creates the tension and the delight.

Women truly are better than men. Otherwise, they'd be intolerable.

ON WOMEN, LOVE, SEX, ET CETERA

You can't belay a man who's falling in love.

Why must love always be accompanied—sooner or later—by sorrow and pain? Why not? Because pure bliss is for pure idiots.

For women, the sexual act is a means to a higher end. For a man, it is an end in itself.

Abolition of a woman's right to abortion, when and if she wants it, amounts to compulsory maternity: a form of rape by the State.

How to Avoid Pleurisy: Never make love to a girl named Candy on the tailgate of a half-ton Ford pickup during a chill rain in April out on Grandview Point in San Juan County, Utah.

Sex is not compulsory, reply the fetus lovers. True: but we're not talking about sex—we're talking about maternity.

The purpose of love, sex, and marriage is the production and raising of children. But look about you: Most people have no business having children. They are unqualified, either genetically or culturally or both, to reproduce such sorry specimens as themselves. Of all our privileges, the license to breed is the one most grossly abused.

Motherhood is an essential, difficult, and full-time job. Women who do not wish to be mothers should not have babies.

A woman, as much as a man, is responsible by the age of forty for the character of her face. But women, obeying the biological imperative, strive harder to preserve a youthful appearance (the reproductive look) and lose it sooner.

If we had the power of ten Shakespeares or a dozen Mozarts, we could not produce anything half so marvelous as one ordinary human child.

It is time for us men to acknowledge not only that women are vastly superior beings (that's easy) but also that they are—in every way that matters—our *equals*. That's hard.

In the end, for all our differences and conflicts, most women and men share the same food, work, shelter, bed, life, joy, anguish, and fate. We need each other.

The feminist notion that the whole of human history has been nothing but a vast intricate conspiracy by men to enslave their wives, mothers, daughters, and sisters presents us with an intellectual neurosis for which we do not yet have a name.

Lifting her skirt, she revealed her treasure. The mother lode. Pretty, I thought, but is it art?

Women who love only women may have a good point.

Homosexuality, like androgyny, might be an instinctive racial response to overpopulation, crowding, and stress. Both flourish when empire reaches its apogee.

I come more and more to the conclusion that wilderness, in America or anywhere else, is the only thing left that is worth saving.

CHAPTER 9

On Nature

Us nature mystics got to stick together.

Nature, like Maimonides said, is mainly a good place to throw beer cans on Sunday afternoons.

Little boys love machines; girls adore horses; grown-up men and women like to walk.

Wilderness begins in the human mind.

I come more and more to the conclusion that wilderness, in America or anywhere else, is the only thing left that is worth saving.

Narrow-minded provincialism: Sad to say but true—I am more interested in the mountain lions of Utah, the wild pigs of Arizona, than I am in the fate of all the Arabs of Araby, all the Wogs of Hindustan, all the Ethiopes of Abyssinia. . . .

No man-made structure in all of American history has been hated so much, by so many, for so long, with such good reason, as that Glen Canyon Dam at Page, Arizona, Shithead Capital of Coconino County.

What draws us into the desert is the search for something intimate in the remote.

If wilderness is outlawed, only outlaws can save wilderness.

The developers and entrepreneurs must somehow be taught a new vocabulary of values.

I'm in favor of animal liberation. Why? Because I'm an animal.

God bless America. Let's save some of it.

Are people more important than the grizzly bear? Only from the point of view of some people.

If people persist in trespassing upon the grizzlies'
territory, we must accept the fact that the grizzlies,
from time to time, will harvest a few trespassers.

All dams are ugly, but the Glen Canyon Dam is sin-
ful ugly.

It is not enough to understand the natural world;
the point is to defend and preserve it.

In the American Southwest, I began a lifelong love
affair with a pile of rock.

Nature is indifferent to our love, but
never unfaithful.

Rocks, like louseworts and snail darters and pupfish
and 3rd-world black, lesbian, feminist, militant
poets, have rights, too. Especially the right to exist.

A true conservative must necessarily be
a conservationist.

In all of nature, there is no sound more pleasing
than that of a hungry animal at its feed. Unless you
are the food.

The industrial corporation is the natural enemy
of nature.

The hawk's cry is as sharp as its beak.

Roosters: The cry of the male chicken is the most barbaric yawp in all of nature.

I'd rather kill a man than a snake. Not because I love snakes or hate men. It is a question, rather, of proportion.

Though men now possess the power to dominate and exploit every corner of the natural world, nothing in that fact implies that they have the right or the need to do so.

Man's deliberate destruction of his own habitat—planet Earth—could serve as a mighty theme for a mighty book worthy of a modern Melville or Tolstoy. But our best fictioneers confine themselves to domestic drama—soap opera with literary trimmings.

There is this to be said for walking: It's the one mode of human locomotion by which a man proceeds on his own two feet, upright, erect, as a man should be, not squatting on his rear haunches like a frog.

Concrete is heavy; iron is hard—but the grass will prevail.

ON NATURE

The world is what it is, no less and no more, and therein lies its entire and sufficient meaning.

The world exists for its own sake, not for ours. Swallow *that* pill!

High technology has done us one great service:
It has retaught us the delight of performing
simple and primordial tasks—chopping wood,
building a fire, drawing water from a
spring. . . .

CHAPTER 10

Science and Technology

You can't study the darkness by flooding it with light.

Pure science is a myth: Both mathematical theoreticians like Albert Einstein and practical crackpots like Henry Ford dealt with different aspects of the same world.

Reason is the newest and rarest thing in human life, the most delicate child of human history.

What is reason? Knowledge informed by sympathy, intelligence in the arms of love.

High technology has done us one great service: It has retaught us the delight of performing simple and primordial tasks—chopping wood, building a fire, drawing water from a spring. . . .

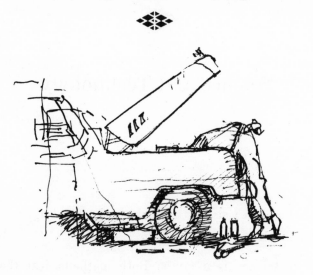

We spend more time working for our labor-saving machines than they do working for us.

The one great gift to humankind from our nuclear physicists has been the nuclear bomb. How can we ever thank them?

Scientific method: There's a madness in
the method.

Science is the whore of industry and the hand-
maiden of war.

Quantum mechanics provides us with an approxi-
mate, plausible, conjectural explanation of what actually is, or was, or may be taking place inside a
cyclotron during a dark night in February.

The mad scientist was once only a creature of
gothic romance; now he is everywhere, busy tortur-
ing atoms and animals in his laboratory.

Those who dream of the joys of living in a space colony should live in a space colony.

The basic science is not physics or mathematics but biology—the study of life. We must learn to think both logically and bio-logically.

Science transcends mere politics. As recent history demonstrates, scientists are as willing to work for a Tojo, a Hitler, or a Stalin as for the free nations of the West.

Generally speaking, it's a matter of only mild intellectual interest to me whether the earth goes around the sun or the sun goes around the earth. In fact, I don't care a rat's ass either way.

What our economists call a depressed area almost always turns out to be a cleaner, freer,
more livable place than most.

CHAPTER 11

Money, Et Cetera

When the biggest, richest, glassiest buildings in town are the banks, you know that town's in trouble.

Most academic economists know nothing of economy. In fact, they know little of anything.

Phoenix, Arizona: an oasis of ugliness in the midst of a beautiful wasteland.

One thing more dangerous than getting between a grizzly sow and her cub is getting between a businessman and a dollar bill.

Industrialism, whether of the capitalist or socialist coloration, is the basic tyrant of the modern age.

Growth for the sake of growth is the ideology of the cancer cell.

The very poor are strictly materialistic. It takes money to be a mystic.

The rich can buy everything but health, virtue, friendship, wit, good looks, love, pride, intelligence, grace, and, if you need it, happiness.

The ever-rising cost of living: Someday soon, the corporate technicians will be locking meters on our noses and charging us a royalty on the air we breathe.

You long for success? Start at the bottom;
dig down.

The real work of men was hunting meat. The inven-
tion of agriculture was a giant step in the wrong
direction, leading to serfdom, cities, and empire.
From a race of hunters, artists, warriors, and tam-
ers of horses, we degraded ourselves to what we are
now: clerks, functionaries, laborers, entertainers,
processors of information.

Daddy, the garbage man is here! Tell him we don't
need any.

Our modern industrial economy takes a mountain
covered with trees, lakes, running streams and
transforms it into a mountain of junk, garbage,
slime pits, and debris.

Wealth should come like manna from heaven, un-
earned and uncalled for. Money should be like
grace—a gift. It is not worth sweating and
scheming for.

In the dog-eat-dog economy, the Doberman is boss.

What our economists call a depressed area almost
always turns out to be a cleaner, freer, more livable
place than most.

Capitalism: Nothing so mean could be right. Greed is the ugliest of the capital sins.

The industrial way of life leads to the industrial way of death. From Shiloh to Dachau, from Antietam to Stalingrad, from Hiroshima to Vietnam and Afghanistan, the great specialty of industry and technology has been the mass production of human corpses.

With the neutron bomb, which destroys life but not property, capitalism has found the weapon of its dreams.

The rich are not very nice. That's why they're rich.

There is no force more potent in the modern world than stupidity fueled by greed.

Nothing could be older than the daily news, nothing deader than yesterday's newspaper.

Among politicians and businessmen, *Pragmatism* is the current term for "To hell with our children."

Business: busyness.

The plow has probably done more harm—in the long run—than the sword.

MONEY, ET CETERA

Money confers the power to command the labor of others. Love of money is love of power. And love of power is the root of evil.

The most common form of terrorism in the U.S.A. is that carried on by bulldozers and chain saws.

Why administrators are respected and school-teachers are not: An administrator is paid a lot for doing very little, while a teacher is paid very little for doing a lot.

All gold is fool's gold.

Everyone should learn a manual trade: It's never too late to become an honest person.

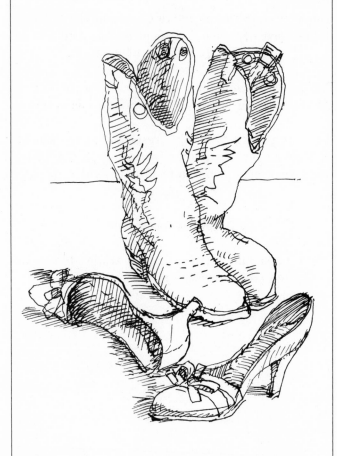

The sexual revolution transformed the American West: Now even cowboys can get laid.

CHAPTER 12

On Cows and Dogs
and Horses

A rancher is a farmer who farms the public lands with a herd of four-legged lawn mowers.

The country dog's report on returning from a first trip to town: "Stand still, they fuck you to death; run and they eat your ass out."

When a man's best friend is his dog, that dog has a problem.

Though I've lived in the rural West most of my life, I never once fell in love with a horse. Not once. Neither end.

Cowboys make better lovers: Ask any cow.

When a dog howls at the moon, we call it religion.
When he barks at strangers, we call it patriotism.

It is not an easy thing to inflate a dog.

A cowboy is a hired hand on the middle of a horse
contemplating the hind end of a cow.

A man without a horse is like a man without a
weapon: stunted and naked.

A cowboy is a farm boy in leather britches and a
comical hat.

The rancher strings barbed wire across the range, drills wells and bulldozes stock ponds everywhere, drives off the elk and antelope and bighorn sheep, poisons coyotes and prairie dogs, shoots eagle and bear and cougar on sight, supplants the native blue-stem and grama grass with tumbleweed, cow shit, cheat grass, snakeweed, anthills, poverty weed, mud and dust and flies—and then leans back and smiles broadly at the Tee Vee cameras and tells us how much he loves the West.

The dog's life is a good life, for a dog.

Man was created to complete the horse.

I wouldn't trade a good horse for the best Rolls-Royce ever made—unless I could trade the Rolls for two good horses.

If you've never ridden a fast horse at a dead run across a desert valley at dawn, be of good cheer: You've only missed out on one half of life.

I always wanted to be a cowboy. But alas! I was burdened early with certain inescapable obligations to world literature.

The sexual revolution transformed the American West: Now even cowboys can get laid.

A landscape, like a man or woman, acquires character through time and endurance.

CHAPTER 13

Places

Page, Arizona, Shithead Capital of Coconino County: any town with thirteen churches and only four bars has got an incipient social problem. That town is looking for trouble.

Places: a cold, bleak, lonely day on the rim at Muley Point, Utah. And the heart-cracking loveliness of this blood-smeared, bitter, incomprehensible slaughterhouse of a world. . . .

England has never enjoyed a genuine social revolution. Maybe that's what's wrong with that dear, tepid, vapid, insipid, stuffy, little country.

I have written much about many good places. But the best places of all, I have never mentioned.

America My Country: last nation on earth to abolish human slavery; first of all nations to drop the nuclear bomb on our fellow human beings.

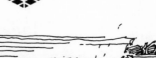

Be it ever so vile, there's no place like home.

A city man is at home anywhere, for all big cities are much alike. But a country man has a place where he belongs, where he always returns, and where, when the time comes, he is willing to die.

A man's duty? To be ready—with rifle or rood—to defend his home when the showdown comes.

The highest treason, the meanest treason, is to deny
the holiness of this little blue planet on which we
journey through the cold void of space.

South of the border: The Hispanics despise the
mestizos, the mestizos look with contempt on *Los In-
dios,* the Indians take it out on their women
and dogs.

The Latino military fare badly when they stumble
into war with the gringos. But in the torture,
murder, and massacre of their own people, they
have always performed with brilliance and elan.

Nearly all of Latin America, from Chile to Mexico,
is one long rack of torture. Financed, equipped, and
refined by the U.S. government.

Alaska is our biggest, buggiest, boggiest state.
Texas remains our largest unfrozen state. But
mountainous Utah, if ironed out flat, would take up
more space on a map than either.

Alaska's chief attractions are: (a) its small and in-
significant human population, thanks to the miserable climate; and (b) its large and magnificent
wildlife population, thanks to (a). Both of these attractions are being rapidly diminished, however, by
(c) the Law of Growth and Space-Age Sleaze.

A VOICE CRYING IN THE WILDERNESS

New Yorkers like to boast that if you can survive in New York, you can survive anywhere. But if you can survive anywhere, why live in New York?

Mexico: where life is cheap, death is rich, and the buzzards are never unhappy.

Finis: *Vox Clamantis in Deserto.*

ABOUT THE AUTHOR

Edward Abbey (1927–1989) was born in Home, Pennsylvania. He received graduate and postgraduate degrees from the University of New Mexico, and attended the University of Edinburgh. He worked for a time as a forest ranger and was a committed naturalist and a fierce environmentalist; such was his anger, eloquence, and action on the subject that he has become a heroic, almost mythic figure to a whole host of environmental groups and literally millions of readers.

Abbey's career as a writer spanned four decades and encompassed a variety of genres, from essays to novels to this volume, which was completed two weeks before his death. One of his early successes was the novel *The Brave Cowboy*, which was made into the movie *Lonely Are the Brave*. His 1968 collection of essays, *Desert Solitaire*, became a necessary text for the new environmentalists, like the group 'Earth First,' and his rambunctious 1975 novel *The Monkey Wrench Gang*, a picaresque tale of environmental guerrilas, which launched a national cult movement and sold over half-a-million copies. Other titles include *The Journey Home*, *Fool's Progress*, and the posthumously released *Hayduke Lives!*

Other Works by Edward Abbey